TOUCH THE
DARKNESS

MARTY GERVAIS

TOUCH THE
DARKNESS

2015 Black Moss Press

Library and Archives Canada Cataloguing in Publication

Gervais, C. H. (Charles Henry), 1946-, author
    Touch the darkness / Marty Gervais.
Poems.
ISBN 978-0-88753-557-4 (paperback)

    I. Title.

PS8563.E7T69 2015   C811'.54   C2015-906909-2

The poems in this collection were written since my appointment in November 2011 as Poet Laureate of the City of Windsor. I am grateful to Benchmark Publishing for publishing many of these in *Modest Denials,* to Biblioasis for others in a chapbook, *Available Light,* to Old Brewery Bay Press for including the Gordon Lightfoot poem in *50+ Poems for Gordon Lightfoot,"* and to Hidden Brook Press for including "Summer in Detroit" in *Window Fishing: The Night We Caught Beatlemania.* I also want to commend Percy Hatfield, the MPP for Windsor-Tecumseh for reading my poetry in the Ontario Legislature in his promotion of a bill to create an Ontario Poet Laureate. I am especially grateful to Cathy Masterson and Christopher Menard of Windsor's Cultural Affairs Office for their efforts in organizing performances of my work at the start of City Council meetings, with the Windsor Symphony Orchestra, on the occasion of the Tall Ships at Windsor's Harbour. Some of these poems, too, were read at Windsor's Negev Dinner, and at Sho Art. I also want to thank the following for their support and inspiration: Peter Hrastovec, Mary Ann Mulhern, Bruce Meyer, Robert Hilles, Susan McMaster, Barry Brodie, John B. Lee, Lorraine Steele, Phil McLeod, Vanessa Shields, Jo-Anne Gignac, Sandi Wheaton, Roger Bryan, and of course, my wife, Donna who has heard all these stories, time and time again.

This book was edited by John B. Lee. The cover illustration is printed with permission from *Shutterstock.* Design is by Jay Rankin.

Published by Black Moss Press at 2450 Byng Road, Windsor, Ontario, N8W 3E8. Canada. Black Moss books are distributed in Canada and the U.S. by Fitzhenry & Whiteside. All orders should be directed there.

Fitzhenry & Whiteside
195 Allstate Parkway
Markham, ON
L3R 4T8

EST.
1969 Black Moss Press

For My Town

CONTENTS

SWEET HOPE

Hands   11

Those First Days   12

To Touch The Sky   14

Sweet Hope   16

The Wedding Dress   19

Summer Nights Outside Metropolitan Hospital   21

The Old Man's War   22

Running From Us   25

Upside Down   29

FUTURE CITY

Planting Pear Trees 300 Years Ago   31

Future City: Thomas Smith, 18th Century Surveyor   32

They Sing To The Sky   34

SIMON GIRTY: 1812 With Nowhere Else To Turn   36

Tecumseh: The Night Before The Capture Of Detroit   38

From The Third Floor of the
Duff-Baby House, Sandwich, Ontario   40

Battle of Stones River, Tennessee:
Death of George 42 Coatsworth (1834-1863)   42

This Man from Detroit —
Survivor of Gettysburg's Iron Brigade   45

The Magistrate's House   47

GEOGRAPHY OF SOLITUDES

Our Canadian Flag Along Detroit's Shore   49

Cathedrals   51

Moments Before the Old Presses
Started At The Windsor Star   53

Stables at Kenilworth Race Track   55

St. Agnes At Rosa Parks/West Grand Blvd.   57

Summer in Detroit   59

Einstein's First Concert   61

Upon Joe Frazier's Death   63

NIGHTS OF WAITING

Porch Spiders   65

Mr. McLuhan And The Windsor Cow   67

Coughing Up Jesus   69

Squatters   71

LAZY BONES

Calling My Father   73

The Timekeeper   75

A Blind Routine   77

Eye To Eye   79

Woman In The Stone Cottage   81

War Widow   83

If I Wrote Your Obit   84

The Barrow   86

Before Noon On Saturday   89

Guardian Angel   91

No Lazy Bones   93

The Underpainting   94

GRACE OF PRAYER

The Innocent   95

RIVER POET

See the river at dusk
— its lake freighters moving with grace and precision
to melodies of coming darkness

Say it like it is
Say it now
Now say it the same

Listen to the man on the street
— his family at midnight bedded down
and children fast asleep

Say it like it is

Hear the slumbering Ferris wheel on the river
— the commotion of muted silence
spinning in the morning light

Say it now

Greet the men and women
who pour out of sprawling factories and shops
heading home to sleep and dream

Now say it the same

Salute the bridge in the morning light
and see how it rouses itself awake
to tell the world it's there, it's there

Say it like it is
Say it now
Now say it the same, the same

Yet why is everyone waiting for the poet
who sings off key
Will he say it now
say it the same

Tell us the reason
Tell us the story

Go and wake the poet
who sings off key
tell him to say it now
say it the same, the same

Will he wake the morning light?
Will he wake the falling day?
Will he wake the dying night?
Will he wake the bridge
and factories, and families lost?

Go and wake the poet
and let him sing off key
hear the raspy heart
that gives him speech

Let him say it now
Say it the same
the same

Let the poet wake the day
Let him walk the night
Let him dance alone
among Ferris wheels
and empty lots and soaring buildings

Let him sing off key
at the edge of sleep

1

SWEET HOPE

HANDS

The first
— those that snatched me
from my mother and lifted me
into the light to my father
in a cold corridor
at Metropolitan Hospital

From that point on,
my life was one of
adult hands — a school nun
gripping my wrist
as she wielded a leather strap,
doctors tilting my chin, palms
flat against my forehead
to find a fever, the priests'
rough hands offering to place
the host upon my gaping tongue,
teachers sliding my fingers
off a page to check the scratchings
of additions and subtractions

and many years later,
my dear mother just before she died
gently cupping my hands
like two tiny doves

assuring me
her hands would bake me a pie

THOSE FIRST DAYS

In these first days of spring
the turmoil of cold
throws off its winter overcoat
to let the light lift high
above barns and silos
that ride the landscape
like boats on the nearby lake

In these first days of spring
I maneuver the rutted roads
the back way to Chatham
past La Paroisse de St. Pierre sur la Tranche
where my mother sang

and marvel at how the tall oaks stretch
like boys stirring in the morning

In these first days of spring
I think of that young farm girl
tiptoeing among frantic birds
in the sunlit henhouse
to gather eggs
while my father paced in the yard
waiting for his new bride

In these first days of spring
I recall my own youth —
reckless nights of drinking
my gut aching
as I rode the trains west
through the mountains
believing in all my fears

In these first days of spring
I drive the river road
the back way to Chatham
past graveyards and levelled fields
I yield to the land
as it trembles like an open palm
ready to gather me in its hold

TO TOUCH THE SKY

There seems to be
no point — the images
all the same, the words
echo in my heart, my
brain bloated with
the jargon of betrayal
of pain, of things
that make no sense
all the whys —
It's all the same
I'm saying it differently
inventing new ways
to tell you how
the hurt thunders
through my veins

I'm a kid
again, standing in
the schoolyard
troubled by
the unkindness of the
nun who scolded me

I climb a tree and
stare into the
classroom below

the nun's dress sways
like a black cloud on
a summer day
as she moves up
and down the aisles

I am hiding from her
in this tall straight maple
high enough to
touch the sky, feel the
blueness sing in my
heart, assured
I can taste the beyond

I perch there
on a steady branch
alone, the weight
of her words lifting
from me

Today I wish
I could climb that tree
to taste the blueness
its purity, its
simplicity, to put
away all this heartache
to be a boy again ...

SWEET HOPE

I sit in my car
by the side of the road
watch the combine
shave this field
of winter wheat
golden and flat
under a dreamy
dark summer sky

I am going
to make some changes

That farmer
will be my grandfather

he will float over
this landscape — straw hat
coveralls, pipe clenched
in his mouth

I will have him
wave to me from
where I sit
at the road's edge

I will shift the barns
and chicken coop
and outhouse
closer to the house
haul out the wagons
and have my grandfather
lead the work horses
into the farm yard

I will put back the oak trees
cut down years ago
in that empty pasture
where we picnicked after church
I will be six again
lumber in a summer storm
and hurry my grandmother
across the yard to shut
the enormous barn doors
against wind and rain

I will put laughter
back into her mouth
as she scoops up my limp body
that has collapsed
abruptly because
the sky has erupted
into sudden thunder

I will paint reflections
in her glasses that show
wind-swept trees
and spooked barn owls
as we race back to the house

I will exchange the words
in my grandfather's frown
as he stands by the back steps
to tell my mother
who has driven an hour
in the still-dark dawn
to hear him say:
"Ta mere est morte"

Instead, my grandmother
will be in the kitchen
loading the wood stove
and turning to my mother
and holding her for that instant

I will stop time
— here and now —
to move all these pieces into place
the perfect farm life
in this imagined game
I will open the eyes
to those I love
and breathe sweet hope
into their limbs and words

I will let prayers
finally have their day

THE WEDDING DRESS

The first time I saw it
I was six
and sunlight spilled
through the bedroom window

I lifted this limp white satiny dress
from a flattened cardboard box
in the cedar chest

I raised it high above my head
— the fitted narrow waist
with a row of fabric-covered buttons
and the invisible side buttons
along the left side seam

Arthur Godfrey on the radio
in the other room
a kettle's whistle
sounds of the man next door
working on the roof of his house

I held the dress high above me
fingers marveling at its smoothness
lost in its whiteness
and the full length skirt
cascading gracefully
in alternating tiers of sheer chiffon

when suddenly my mother's voice
at the doorway told me
it was a summer day like this
at the farm in Stoney Point
when first she put on the dress

how she had run upstairs
to the room shaded by the front yard maple

how she remembered
gleaming cars zigzagged in the yard
and her fingers fidgeted
as she slipped on this lacy dress
—the day was hot and cloudless
and her father complained
there hadn't been enough rain
and she told me she had waited
forever resting on the edge of the bed
for her mother to come and approve
and sat staring out the window
shoes resting beneath her
like two sleeping birds
on the hardwood floor

then heard her mother's voice
at the edge of the room
softness of words enveloping her
in that moment

and she knew it was time
to take the car to the church
its steeple towering above the flatness
of farm fields

and she wondered then
if it was all a mistake

SUMMER NIGHTS OUTSIDE METROPOLITAN HOSPITAL

I saw my grandmother in the back bedroom
of her little house
She was dying of stomach cancer
I was 10 —
By summer she was
on the third floor of the hospital
I'd visit with my father
but my sister and I had to wait
in the car
We'd roll on the backseat of a sprawling Plymouth
making ugly faces and laughing
or trying to guess which window was hers
We'd wait and wait until my father
would stroll out in the humid twilight air
with ice cream and ice-cold Vernors

After a while we didn't care
about my grandmother
We longed to be pampered
Every day begging our father
to take us to the hospital
We promised to wait by the curb
wait the hours out
for the treats

It all stopped when
my grandmother died

We missed the ice cream

THE OLD MAN'S WAR

The bookshop owner believed
I was blind
I stood in the shop
struggling to make out
the words of De Gaulle's memoirs
reading them in French
I was 14
I had just come from
the optometrist
and the drops in my eyes
continued to plague my sight

I was reading about
the Resistance
and De Gaulle's old mentor Marshal Pétain
reading about betrayal
the decision to save
the aging war hero
who was condemned to death
the decision to exile him
to a windswept island
in the Bay of Biscay

The man in the bookshop
asked if there was a problem
because I held the book
so close to my eyes

I liked the idea
that he believed I was blind
though I never said
anything to suggest this
I went on reading
shaking my head

in modest denials
making him feel sorry for me

I remember this now
as I sit in this café
in the Latin Quarter in Paris
and read that someone
has discovered
one street in France
still named after Pétain
in Tremblois
near the Belgian border
— the last town bearing
the former war hero's appellation
soon to be renamed
Rue de la Belle-Croix

A year ago another town
removed a painting of Pétain
from the town hall
I think about this old soldier
called "conqueror of Verdun"
his last days
on the Atlantic coast
a spare two-room bunker
his wife daily walking
from a nearby hotel
to sit and share a meal
and the roll and groan
of the Atlantic just beyond

I remember reading about
his coffin being dug up
and driven across the
country to Paris
where it was later
found abandoned in a garage

Now the modest sign
for *Rue Pétain* marking a street
a mere 600 feet long
is being taken down
sixty years after his death

I wonder about the man
whose final request was
a bottle of water
from Lourdes

RUNNING FROM US

My first —
was a Shepherd
my brother brought home
from the Navy
We kept *Gunner* two weeks
before dropping him off at the farm
and my uncle finally shot him
in the head for raiding the chicken coop
The second—
a Springer Spaniel
That's when we lived in the country
and *Sybil* chased cars
as they rounded the bend
near our house
and sometimes she trailed after
the tractor in sweeping fields
of winter wheat
but when we brought her
to the city
she wandered off
was sideswiped by a car
and languished in a drainage ditch
before being disposed off
by the Humane Society
The third —
a Scotty named *Ezra*
after the poet
whines at every recitation
of Ginsberg's "Howl"
was killed in the middle
of rush hour on a city street
and we wrapped her in a blanket
and buried her in the backyard
The fourth —

the newspaper's pet-of-the-week
Oscar was a digger
discovering ways to flee
the yard and raid
neighbourhood garbage cans
I'd chase her down with my car
till she'd give up
scramble into the back seat
and ride home with me
sitting up regally
fish breath
smart-alecky eyes
happy smirk on her face
Then one winter I didn't notice
she had sneaked outside
and found shelter
underneath my car
and I backed up
felt something dragging
and cursed, believing my son
had forgotten a hockey bag
on the driveway
That's when I heard her
— caught under my tires
legs broken, spine crushed
The fifth —
a Cairn Terrier
who wouldn't roll over or sit up
and had everything backwards
running from us when we called
running to us
when we told her to stay
The breeder warned us
Coco would never be a show dog
— her head too small
That should've been a tipoff

Coco never barked
never jumped up on anyone
never complained
never actually did anything
but sleep and laze
under the pear tree
among Lilly of the Valley
in our backyard
Yesterday morning, she ambled
along the pool's edge
in warm sunlight
daydreaming, lost
in philosophical pursuits
only a dog could hope to solve
and stumbled and slipped
into the water
that had collected
on the winter pool cover
and we had forgotten
about her, having
welcomed home a son
from across the ocean
Then realized - too late -
Coco hadn't returned
I found her at midnight
floating like a shroud
or a soaken rug
at the water's edge
and lifted her stiffened body
gently to the pool deck
The next day
we wrapped her
in a threadbare towel
placed her in a cardboard box
dug a hole
under the pear tree

and stood as a family
bare-headed in the rain

The next morning
when I was working
I saw *Coco*
idling in the hallway
as she sometimes did
I swear she was there
and looked again
and again

UPSIDE DOWN

It's not a happy face
the shape of this shoreline of ours

maybe it's because
we're upside down
looking north instead of south
like the rest of the country

maybe we haven't learned
to smile so readily —
our weakness betrayed
in that frown

I first heard this
from the nuns in Riverside
at the school two blocks
south of the river

and with my buddies,
we'd slip down
past the heavy sewer grates
and wend our way
underground
down to the shoreline
soaken ankles, wet shoes and pant legs
and emerge wide-eyed
to Detroit's dark smoke-rising signals
that blackened the blue sky

We were a band of boys pretending
to be Tecumseh or Simon Girty
or John Wayne or Gene Autry

The nuns in Riverside said
we were the upside down people

Maybe that's why we did our crazy cartwheels
along the solitary riverbank —
saluting the Americans to the north

2

FUTURE CITY

PLANTING PEAR TREES 300 YEARS AGO

The black robes arrived in late spring
long sprawling canoes
hugging the bend in the river

till they spotted men and women
waving from the south bank

and came ashore bearing gifts
and pear tree seedlings from France

The fathers planted the trees
in groups of twelve —

setting only one apart like the apostle

All these years later
one survives in a field by
the mouth of the river

solitary, alone, exiled
its tired drooping branches
stretching for repose in the black soil

planted there 300 years ago
to bear fruit, to bear truth

FUTURE CITY: THOMAS SMITH, 18ᵀᴴ CENTURY SURVEYOR

He loved the light —
it made the darkness glow
on nights when he scrambled
down the embankment
to the birch canoe
summer moon high above
its face swimming
in the river below —
paddle in the darkness
breaking the silence
burning fires along
the shore, the noise of day
raging in his head
among rigid visions of roads
and buildings and merchants
and farmers

In that moment returning
to the south shore
he dreamt of home, the River Wye
its torrent through the valley
in early spring
his mind swarming back then
with drawings of ancient streets
imagining the noise of day
of people with purpose

Now here along this river
there was only his canoe
in the swift current of darkness
that took him back —

only a compass, a set

of plotting instruments
and stiff rolled up drawings
in a leather portfolio
and its secrets emerging
in the inked geometry
of avenues not yet known

He loved the night
he loved the light
that made the darkness glow

THEY SING TO THE SKY

On the Occasion of the Tall Ships in Windsor

I hear them sing sea shanties
on long summer days
Topsail schooners and brigantines and brigs
I feel them drift to the sky
full of heartache and dismay
I see these ghostly vessels

I hear their songs
amid spinnaker sails
Topmasts, Square rigs, ketches and sloops
I see them sway
like mirrors of the sea
these solitary yawls
lightweight and taller
I feel them nudge the horizon
and grow dim, and sway
as they skim
across a cloud-drifted lake

I hear them sing sea shanties
on long summer days
fearing faltering three-masted sails
fearing wind, sudden, and picking up
as we hurry to lash down gratings
and cuss looming 12-foot swells
as we dip and plummet headlong
into wet rain like jilted brides

I hear them sing
sea shanties on long summer days
flimsy ketches and sloops and cutters
I see them reef the small sails
as wind mounts a terrible refrain
They sing for this storm
with sullen disdain

I hear them sing
sea shanties on long summer days
simple barges and dinghies and staysail schooners
They sing for the moon
in its flight to deny
They sing till the sea
melts into the sky

SIMON GIRTY: 1812 WITH NOWHERE ELSE TO TURN

By 70, he was nearly blind
and each afternoon would make his way
on horseback along the river road
to drink and tell stories
at his favourite public house
owned by a friend

By nightfall, he was done in
and someone would help him
to his horse and it would take him back
to the farm at the mouth of the Detroit

He cared nothing for war
except for the fields and the corn
he sold to the army

Or that's what he'd tell the men
who drank with him
and no one dared interrupt
— after all, was he not the one who burned
an American militiaman at the stake?
Did he not dangle enemy scalps
from his belt?

Or that's what he'd tell the men
at night when they'd surround his table
and lean in close to learn
if all the tales were true
and why the great Shawnee chief
had joined him on the farm
at the edge of town
or maybe they wanted to know
if he feared the Americans crossing the river

or what it was like to finish off
a man who begged for mercy

But the old blind Indian guide dismissed them
again saying he cared nothing for war
nothing for death except to vow
he'd be buried along the river
and curse any American
for digging him up

Or that's what he would tell the men

Then he'd push his way past
the rowdy pub, and lurch out into the cold
where his horse rested in the night
and he'd ride home, often dozing off
under a moonlight sky, fearing nothing
not even the darkness

And maybe deep down
was sorry, and mourned the loss
of a brother and the death of his family

And maybe *hate* was always there

But he cared nothing for war
and what it left him when
there was nowhere else to turn

Or that's what he'd tell the men

TECUMSEH: THE NIGHT BEFORE
THE CAPTURE OF DETROIT

What could he have known
the night before
when he slipped outside
beyond the camp and down the
river's edge

deerskin coat and fringed pantaloons
and walking where fate would take him
past sleeping soldiers and
wakeful sentries

What could he have known
amidst fires burning
by the open water
or pacing the river's bank
to study the rigid stroke
of shoreline darkness

or seeing the British general
scratching out the terms of surrender
in the lighted house upon the hill
the night before

What could he have known
of the morning ahead
rousing from troubled sleep
to voices of cannons
in the stilled air of an August dawn

What could he have known
of a river's mist swallowing them
in such eerie silence
and the blood of his blood
thundering into a battlefield
less than a mile away

What could he have known

FROM THE THIRD FLOOR OF THE DUFF-BABY HOUSE, SANDWICH, ONTARIO

I stand at a north window
on the third floor
of this stately house
imagine families
crossing the river in winter cold
hauling supplies
loaded up on sleds

refugees of war
desperate for shelter, food, warmth

seeking that one thin horizontal line
of eerie silence stretched
across a flat skyline —
courthouse, church steeple, graveyard

and hear curses and laughter
in the icy British stillness

I imagine soldiers dining here
in frivolous candle light
fretting over a morning assault
fearing traitors and spies and assassins
feeling spooked by a cold January moon

From this third floor
I imagine men and women and children
slipping across a windswept river
with daytime collapsing all around
yet somehow lifting themselves
despite this meddlesome burden of fear

Then suddenly I wake from my reverie
to the carpenters
hammering down the roof
from a cannonball
that crashed through
in a battle that won nothing
for nobody

BATTLE OF STONES RIVER, TENNESSEE: DEATH OF GEORGE COATSWORTH (1834-1863)

I must have driven those roads
in winter months
a thousand times or more
following narrow ribbons
that crisscrossed stubbled open fields
where the sky dips down
to drink a slumbering alluvial landscape

and it never occurred to me
that among the dead
in the cemetery at a forgotten crossroad
was that of a soldier
a surgeon who had run off
to join the 88th Illinois Regiment

this man needed among his own
both at home but also
in a war to the south

And how on those frosty mornings
a hundred years later
I paced the creaky wooden floors
of the old post office to collect the mail —
impatient to get on with my day

and never once heard the story
of George Coatsworth who promised
his wife, Stella, he'd be back in spring
after signing up for Sherman's army

this man needed among his own
both at home but also
in a war to the south

I thought of this man's spouse packing up
a picnic lunch and guiding the children
down to the lake, a good hike
carefully negotiating her way
over the steep decline
to Erie's summer shore

I imagined Stella sitting in sunlight
praying for word, a letter
as the children cooled
from August's long humid days

this man needed among his own
both at home but also
in a war to the south

It wasn't until after the first snowfall
after the start of the New Year 1863
that she received word

Maybe she spotted Tom, the postmaster
riding in a windy open carriage
his horse trotting one morning
over that same icy concession road —
news of his death, typhoid

Stella wasted no time boarding a train
then four days on a stage coach
that wound its way
deep into Tennessee
before taking a month to track back
through rebel lines
to return her beloved's body

and read Col. Sherman's letters
about that winter day when
in frenzied cold before the battle
"everything was still ...
before the terrible work of death began"

and wrote about
this man barely 30
needed among his own
both at home but also
in a war to the south

As I stand before a modest headstone
I think of Stella's prayers
carrying the weight of his death
— all sadness and anger
bound up in sheets that wrapped his body
how she must have felt his stillness
that lay in a wooden casket
she ferried across Lake Erie

Here was a man needed among his own

THIS MAN FROM DETROIT — SURVIVOR
OF GETTYSBURG'S IRON BRIGADE

The night before he went into battle
he folded and tucked a letter away
into lining of his soft-brimmed black hat
—riots in his city back home,
homes burned, two dead

The night before he went into battle
he sat among his own of the 24th Michigan brigade
far back of Cemetery Hill
Confederate fires burning in the distance
and read his mother's words
worried over the next day's charge
and the hell-for-leather image of George Armstrong Custer
circling on the field
leading his men into the smoky fray

The night before he went into battle
fearful, yet never guessing he'd be trailing closely
on the heels of the 2nd Wisconsin
sprinting so fast there was no time to reload
the muzzle-loaded rifle

The night before he went into battle
he felt terribly alone, slumped under a star-lit sky wondering
when he might stroll freely the flattened land
outside the city up north
No hero that night, this tired young soldier in a wool jacket
blisters in boots a size too large

The night before he went into battle
he dreamt of waking with dawn breaking over the trees
and glint of iron weaponry in looming stillness
and swore the men charging into that new day

ran barefoot and scared
but no longer angry

THE MAGISTRATE'S HOUSE

For Alexander Bartlet and Thomas Hines

Sometimes I go out
in early morning
cruising up and down Windsor streets
in search of his house
—its sprawling Georgian verandah
the usual sash windows
sturdy front door with transom
and sidelights

They've moved it, but not far
I've narrowed it down
to two or three —
In a way I don't want to know
I want to paint my own story
of that that morning: 1865
of the billy-goat bearded town clerk
racing down a flight of stairs
to the landing —
paperboys fanning out into Ferry Street
from the ferry docks
a cold Easter Monday
the boys shouting "Lincoln Shot!"

I see the magistrate's frown
in the dim April dawn
his voice summoning the boys
to bring him the paper
spy him pausing there in the gaping entrance
wondering what went wrong
a civil war across the river
the flight of slaves to his shores
now rumours of John Wilkes Booth
making his own run across the river

That Easter Monday
a sleepy town rouses itself awake
to the scuttlebutts
of a ferry boat captain
who stopped at nothing to spin the legend
of being held at gunpoint
by Lincoln's assassin
and the magistrate sorts out
the hearsay down by the docks
wind howling up that street
sweeping its way into the
shopkeepers' doorways
on that spit-gray day

It's all gone now but for that story
and the ramshackle house
that sleeps somewhere
quietly breathing

telling no one
the truth

3

GEOGRAPHY OF SOLITUDES

OUR CANADIAN FLAG ALONG DETROIT'S SHORE

For Peter Hrastovec

If you stand still
you will hear its faint voice
born in winter commotion,
in smoky partisan committee rooms
sprawling auditoriums
Legion halls, and
hallowed parliamentary corridors

You will hear all the good
all the bad, all the everywhere outcry

That was just a little of us
forever trying to make sense
of history, tradition ... and political ego

But its voice was clear—
Let's do the right thing
Let's do it now
Let's hear me sing

A half century later
we sport two broad red borders
like strong shoulders
symmetrical and straight and proud
hugging a single leaf

And here along this river
we might call this a map of anywhere
where the leaf flutters on water
in a peaceful geography of coupling solitudes

I can't help but hear its song calling
This is ours, that is yours
I'll let you see me now
Across the distant shores

CATHEDRALS

They were cathedrals
—these sprawling factories
with frosted glass metal-framed windows
that tilted open to a landscape
of wartime houses and brick schools
—the workers, like monks, moved
in slow motion, and my father
in a white shirt and crooked bowtie
paced among them
worried over meeting the numbers

Today, these places lie mute —
edifices of crumbling brick
cracked and broken windows
and the rubble-strewn earth
wrestling back the 20th century
with trees bursting up
through the busted concrete

Months before my father died
we cruised the empty streets
and picked our way among the ruins
of the grand old Studebaker and Ford plants
the Motor Lamp on Seminole,
boarded up dry goods stores
and barber shops and fish & chip joints

We stood in the middle of the sunlight floor
of the place where he made headlamps —
an acre of concrete once complicated
by conveyor belts and sturdy steel columns

and he told me of those mornings
walking to work from Albert Road

chomping on an apple
a metal lunch pail tucked under his arm
a skinny boy of 16 having landed here
from the mining towns in the north
a job on the line, a job he'd never quit
till his heart gave out
Now there are mornings when I pause
before a single building
and peer through a gap-tooth wall
of cracked glass windows
imagining life on that concrete floor

remember him saying he'd trade everything
to return to that time of sweet independence
of youth, a job and a cheque on Fridays

MOMENTS BEFORE THE OLD PRESSES
STARTED AT THE WINDSOR STAR

The first thing you'd see were
the hands, gloved and ink-stained
then the faces of men dwarfed by
the three-storied leviathan that sprawled out
in the morning ready to rouse and rise

You'd eye the pressmen pacing the perimeter
of this giant and see them stretch long clean sheets
of paper from giant rolls through its idle frame

They knew the monster well and knew
to wait and knew to hear its glory

I used to slide down from the newsroom
to stand nearby and watch, and hear the voices
over the faint growl of this prodigious creature
I'd see them carrying heavy metal plates
clamping them into place, and watch them fit
the curved cylinders to its pulsating contours
— catch the slow mumble among
the men as they moved to feed the beast
to make it come alive, to make it stir

They knew the monster well and knew
to wait and knew to hear its glory

These were the men clambering at dawn
among tiered platforms and galleries
built around this slumbering creature
— the first to spot the headlines
to read the world upside down and backwards

They knew the monster well and knew
to wait and knew to hear its glory

STABLES AT KENILWORTH RACE TRACK

That day driving out
to the tumbledown stables
south of the city
I knew nothing of that moment in October 1920
I'd gone there with a woman I'd met at a bookstore
— horseback riding late, late afternoon
straw and dust and manure
the sharp odour of Absorbine
and tobacco and seeing
threadbare plaid blankets folded over
the gates in the horse barn
and the final rays of sunlight
pouring into the stalls
I watched this quiet elderly man leading the horses
out to the yard, the rich chestnut slope of their beauty
accentuated by the late fall's light

I knew nothing of that moment so long ago
but think of it now, too late,
and realize this man was there —
a boy among the stables
fetching straw and oats
his milky blue eyes and boyish hands
guiding the horses
into the silent moonlit yard at dawn

I want him to be there again with the great ones
—the race of the century
Man O'War and *Sir Barton*

I want him to be at edges, slipping past
with pails of clean water
to sense the stillness of the stall

where motionless Man O'War stood
—they say Big Red, as he was called,
 was so beautiful it made you want to cry
and say his very stillness was that
of a coiled spring, a crouched tiger
I want to believe Big Red scared the boy
that first morning in the fall
Yet I knew nothing of that day in October
when I drove out to those timeworn stables
where this boy once stood in awe
of men who kept watch over the great stallion

I knew nothing of the track we rode on
at twilight where Big Red once galloped
like a nightmare roaring into history
I wished now I had paid attention
I wished I had remembered what
this man looked like, what he might've said
I wished now we could've talked

Instead, I sat perched on a broken down mare
trotting along a track I knew nothing about
trailing after a new girlfriend
thinking only of her
and my next move

ST. AGNES AT ROSA PARKS/WEST GRAND BLVD.

As night falls, the crack addicts
gather in the abandoned church
at Rosa Parks and West Grand
and piece by piece
they have begun
to dismantle the organ
in the choir loft,
ripping out the wood
to feed a mounting bonfire
on the concrete floor —

the towering gothic windows
of St. Agnes bow above
like melancholic ghosts
eager to warm themselves
welcoming these strangers

Someone is singing

I hear them inside
see the fluttering glow
from the windows
hear laughter
broken words of a chorus
lifting in the fading light
of twilight

I see the skeletal tree's tangle
of shapes lurching in my path
along an uneven walkway
to the side door of the church

hear the crackling of fire
alighting the graffiti-scarred walls

imagine a cluster
of men and women
huddling in the cold

I decide to turn back
to the street, back
to my locked car

Seconds before departing
I swear that in the hushed
gloom of the church
I hear the whir
of its big ceiling fans
or maybe wings starting up
coming alive
as voices of adoration and fear
fill the sullen silence of
this wintry city night

SUMMER IN DETROIT

A flimsy wooden seat
from Detroit's old Olympia
bought for $25 is the closest thing I have
to the Beatles who played in that arena
once in 1964, again in 1966
and I think of my friend
who said it was nearly midnight
when their Greyhound pulled away
from the Olympia —
the Fab Four singing *Long Tall Sally*
from the open windows of the bus
with teenage girls rushing after them into the street
Cleveland bound, an all-nighter

Someone said they heard their laughter
saw them wave on that humid August night
swore they tossed their cufflinks
to frantic stretched-out hands

My 18-year-old high school buddy
had skipped class
to hang out at the Whittier Hotel downtown
and dialed all day long a radio station
in hopes of winning one square inch
of the sheets Lennon slept on

I don't know if any of it is true
I don't care — the broken down
seat from the Olympia
rests in a corner of my basement

I'm struggling to find some kind of metaphor
for how I should feel, some lyric moment
for this brush with greatness

as I settle down on that wooden chair
the hum of the furnace
in the silence of a summer afternoon
but this is nothing to compare
with the postage stamp-sized remnant
from John Lennon's bed
that rests in a dresser drawer
in an envelope from the radio station

I swear I can hear someone sleeping

EINSTEIN'S FIRST CONCERT

A friend of a friend
had an uncle in Detroit
who remembers
Albert from the winter of 1934

how he meticulously
packed up his violin
before making his way
out to the blue Buick
to drive from Princeton
to Fifth Street New York

This uncle drove with Albert
— the two in the same orchestra
both violinists
Their first recital
226 paying patrons
Bach's concerto for two violins

This uncle spoke about
Albert's narrow fingers
lifting the instrument
lightly from the case
the bow next
his routine set
a formula of repetition
movement so predictable
as to be perfect
and hopeful as prayer

Albert's eyes danced in
the light of the concert hall
when those first notes rose
and came alive

every sound finding
its place in the silence

Nothing had escaped this man
— not even backstage radiators
hissing their envy

UPON JOE FRAZIER'S DEATH

Based on interview with Carl Fussman 2004

I lived by the body shot

My dad
was missing his left hand
and part of his left forearm

I don't know what happened
I never asked

I heard another man
tried to kill him
in an argument
over a woman

I wish I knew now
I never asked

But I got the roof of that left hook
as a boy from pulling
a big cross-saw with my dad
He'd use his right hand
so I had to use my left

I lived by the body shot

My mom? When
your mom dies
so do you... he told me

I never asked why

Health? You have a
lot of tools in that body —

liver, kidneys, lungs
You soften that up
and see what happens

I lived by the body shot

Medals? I cut up my
Olympic gold into 11 pieces —
gave all 11 of my kids a piece

...It'll come together again
when they put me down

They'll live by my body shot

4

NIGHTS OF WAITING

PORCH SPIDERS

For Calder

For weeks
I have studied them —
at dusk they commence their work
— spinneret magic
fashioning an intricate silken gallery of traps
for their prey

in this night of waiting

first the safety line
then a web of sticky silk
that snags and snares
these bold intruders

I watch these wily orb-weavers
in a night of waiting
feel their patience tested
through a sleepy night
as they doze in silence
dreaming of feasting on everything
that nudges their invisible wall

There's no escaping —
in this night of waiting

They sense the vibration of an interloper —
a trespasser having blundered blindly
into its neighbourhood —

In an instant, they leap lightly
through the radial scaffolding
eight eyes, eight legs, sharp fangs
racing for the kill

I wait for these wily orb-weavers
to spin their victims
dress them for death
and wrap them tightly in fine silk

There's no escaping
in this night of waiting

Dinner is served

MR. MCLUHAN AND THE WINDSOR COW

Maybe this is what McLuhan thought
when he happened upon
this daydreaming cow
as she trotted
with such thoughtless abandon into
that country road

What was she doing
when there was
nothing else to do?

Conjuring better pastures
maybe ruminating
about meandering into a nearby parking lot
among open car windows
longing for a spot
to snoop and maybe snooze
under a blue Windsor sky

picturing what it might be like
to slip into the back seat
of an old Chevrolet
and doze away the day

There's nothing to do as usual
so why not wander
weary of all that cow inertia
and step out from the others
and leave behind
their annoying bovine gossip
in the lazy humid air

maybe step aside from
that tired list of silly names
Mr. Farmer has christened them:
Devilish Delilah, Crafty Caroline
Pain-in-the-Arse Mary-Rose
and *Ooola-la Ola*

There's nothing to do as usual
so why not wander
where the grass is greener

and why not move gracefully
past the open gate
into that ribbon of road
and break free of the regime
of every day

abandon cow passivity
leave behind a staring crowd

and finally be the girl you always
imagined on those tiresome
going-nowhere days

COUGHING UP JESUS

It was the day
my dog ate baby Jesus —
this wiry Jack Russell
knocking the Advent Calendar
to the floor
and rooting out the chocolates
one by one
till the 25th

and Jesus was gobbled up
in that toothy slobbery
mouth of my dog
and the month
wasn't even done—
two weeks still to Christmas
and my dog hacked up Jesus
all up in one rushed instant,
a gooey puddle
sliding like a dark shadow
over the gleam and twinkle
of Yuletide decorations

It was that kind of day

every year the priest
prattling on about
the real meaning
of Christmas
about putting an end
to godless buying
about putting "Christ"
back into Christmas

and maybe that's
what my Jack Russell
had in mind when
he coughed up
the sacred and divine

SQUATTERS

I get out of bed
to see them cavorting
on my front lawn
at not quite 5 a.m.

a mother skunk
and four furry tailed
little ones
frolicking in the moonlight

I regard them
the way others might judge
squatters, or worse,
carjackers

I fear them
I can't say anything

I feel trapped
in my own house
not wanting to risk
making my early morning
run to *Tim Hortons*

yet I wish to warn these creatures
what might befall them
if they dare burrow
under my pool

Last summer
their hillbilly cousins
moved in

I hired a wildlife service
to trap them humanely
then fed a hose
down their tunnels
blocking up escape routes
with cement blocks
hoping to roust them
from their home
but they never got the point —

they defied my every move
till I stuffed
their underground grid
with chlorine-loaded pool pucks
and sealed up the exits

Now I want to tell
these happy little creatures
mind your own business
leave me alone
let me go to my car...
pretty please

5

LAZY BONES

CALLING MY FATHER

I came across
my father's old phone number
scrawled in the address book

—the numbers rolled off
so easily, the times
I called with
a piece of good news

or that moment
in late spring
when I telephoned
to tell my father
his son, my brother
was dying and
we had better
get down to the hospital

or the call I made
from Vancouver
when I was 20
and needed train fare
to return home
and heard
impatience
in my father's
gravelly voice

I sat and stared
at the number
for a long time
then dialed

letting it ring and ring
wondering if
I should hang up
if suddenly
a stranger answered

Deep down
I innocently hoped
someone
might pick it up
in Heaven

THE TIMEKEEPER

My father told me of a man
from the factory—
how after he retired
as the company's timekeeper
he never knew what time
it was — or sorry
that's not exactly true

He told me of this man
who had a dozen broken clocks
in his house
all registering a different time
and he'd go from room to room
scratching his head
wondering over the truth
till he decided it didn't matter
— the clocks were wrong
and he'd set them
all at the same hour
never bothering to find out
what the real time was

After a day or two
the hands of the clocks
grew weary and slow
and once again
were out of sync
with one another
and the man would smile
and regard them as old friends
all pacing their time
some running fast, some slow
some no longer caring
to keep up

But the man was patient
and he'd set them all over again
going from room to room
caring for them like stray cats

My father told me
when finally the man died
at home in his bed
the ambulance attendant
scanned the room
to record the time of death

and all the ticking clocks
began to chime in unison

A BLIND ROUTINE

Mornings when my father leaves the house
he bids her goodbye —
tells her where he's going
what he's doing
and why —

and swears he hears her
moving about the kitchen
though she passed away
a year and a half ago

He cares not to see
refuses to walk with a white cane —
his world a blur
a slowing pace

Mornings my father leaves
tucking bank books into
bulging pockets
shuffles to the street
to a nearby plaza
paces outside the bank
waiting for it to open

My father has not forgotten
what he promised her
why he's there
and finally slips behind a desk
and directs the clerk
to scan the columns
recite its debits and balances
He nods and bids
the kind woman — adieu
His world a blur

a slowing pace —
of greetings and goodbyes

My father has not forgotten
the weight of keys
in his pocket for a
car he no longer owns
Some afternoons
he falls asleep in a chair
cupping the keys
to the 1966 black *Cutless Supreme*
dreaming familiar streets,
coasting past crumbling bygone factories
or a wind-swept river
of his youth

The only safe bet
my father knows
are the prescription bottles
on a nearby dresser

He lives for tomorrow

EYE TO EYE
After Surgery On My Left Eye

They are twin brothers
suddenly fighting for attention
inside my head
the better one miserable
about having now failed me
the other dancing
like a fool in an open field
happy in his new notoriety
I want to ask
What do you see?
But the two squabble continuously
paying me no heed
lost in tenacious claims
eager to be alone, free
luxuriating in pure autonomy
What do you see?
I demand over and over again
as I make my way
down winding dark staircases
along glaring sun-drenched streets
I need your help
I complain as I slip into a car
to drive across town
worried sick about my safety

One eye finally relinquishes
all concerns, but only for the moment
as he surveys the road itself
and pauses to warn me of the passage
how close the curb is
the colour of lights ahead

Meanwhile the other is off on his own
spots a park where
someone is walking a dog
life is dreamy, solitary
who needs anyone else —
live for the moment
What do you see?
I want to know
but neither is speaking to me
as I zigzag fretfully into the future
uncertain of the very curve of the earth
sensing how my two impetuous sons
try to outdo one another
as they anxiously preen and pirouette
before one another
troubled over whether the world is
actually looking
at them

WOMAN IN THE STONE COTTAGE

For Pat Sturn At Age 100

This morning
I woke from a dream
wherein I was carrying
your cane —
the one you used to hang
over the door handle
to the kitchen

I saw you use it
maybe once
when you asked my wife
to accompany you
on a tour of
your tiny stone cottage

Why was I carrying it?
Or did I? It floated before me
awkwardly out of reach

This morning
I woke from a dream
and the sky above was
a sickly tornado green
wind picking up
and the cane skipped
along like an impetuous child
in front of me

I couldn't keep up
Where was it taking me?

This morning
I woke from a dream
and you were rushing
along in the garden
behind the cottage
and I was trying to follow
with that silly cane
When did your feet
get so fast,
skirt tails fluttering
and you glancing over
your shoulder

Where were you taking me?

I saw you float high above
the rooftops like
a figure out of Chagall
desperate in
my clambering
among chimneys
and the patchwork of shingles

I tried to wake from
that dream hoping
the cane was firmly
in my hand
to take me back
to take me there

WAR WIDOW

She bade him goodbye
at the train station down by the river —
in those last seconds before
he stepped onto the train

and ran her right hand
awkwardly over the wool lapel of his uniform
pretending to smooth out a wrinkle

Years later she would tell me
I knew he wasn't coming back

She had been married two months
a son growing within her

She bound his letters from the war
with a red elastic band
and tucked them into a dresser drawer

Years later when she married again
there were times when
she would slip these out
and sit for an afternoon
and read them

struggling to make sense
of those years
as a young widow with a baby son

in whose eyes she saw
a stolen future

IF I WROTE YOUR OBIT

For John B. Lee

As we sweep a tangle of branches
away from the gaping entrances
and step boldly into the cold barns
that sit abandoned
like bad children
I wonder what I might write
about you if I live to see you die

I see two dusty smocks
left dangling on a hook
those of the hired hand
a friend of your father's
dead now maybe 40 years
never taken down

Surely, you don't expect him
to return this gray winter day

Sometimes when I look at you
I see your father
— maybe in the way you lean
on the wooden gate
breath steaming the air
as you speak about
those who peopled this farm

I wonder if deep down
you sense betrayal
in your decision
to pack a bag
at that end of a summer day —
eager eyes seeking city streets
limbs lifting and departing
wind sweeping open fields
or how you rose at dawn to care for lambs
or rode the pickup into town

Do you sense the wrong?
Do you wake wondering
what might've been?
Do you walk into these
tumble-down barns
where nature is doing all it can
to shrug off the weight
of that history?

Did it occur to you
that you might slip on
those tattered coats
that hang in the barn?

THE BARROW

His work boots are carefully lined up
under a narrow wooden table
fat jars of anise
bake in the morning sunlight
a calendar with a partly naked woman
hangs near an open window
and time has stopped at November
though it's now July
Denis today is wearing a shirt
not like when we met him
on the sloping field down the road
where his truck was parked
and where he kept a jug of wine
He was full of smiles then
and his large hands gestured
to the sweep of vines
row by row as though
they were his students
in a classroom
Today he settles down
at a table in the sunlight
and pours us a drink
and wants to tell us about his pig
and the chickens he keeps
but it is the pig he wants us
to see and guides us
along the gravel pathway
to the barn and unlatches
the heavy wooden door
and the light
of the afternoon floods
the doorway
and Denis steps inside —
his pig circling in the pen

like an excited family dog
Denis stands to one side
as if he is introducing a wife
or a girlfriend and it occurs to me
the woman who earlier placed the glasses
on the table in the garden
was his girlfriend and
he never introduced her
before she took his keys
and drove off in his truck
but here we are with his pig
her flat snout
stretching for our affection
and Denis is proud in this moment
standing to one side
in the cool darkness of the hot day
This man who speaks
about politics, the rules
the levies on his business
and says the secret is
to keep things simple
hide under the radar
find a way around
make things work out
I imagine at night
before he shuts the door
and returns
to the modest house
he reaches down
and tells the pig
everything that's
on his mind
— disagreements
with municipal bureaucrats
—a woman who visits
each day to have lunch

—neighbours who scorn
his eccentric ways
—and why not tell the pig
the pig sees him
and paces the pen
happy to hear his voice
and never disagrees
and believes him
to be right and wise
and is always there
to bid him goodnight

BEFORE NOON ON SATURDAY

It was just before noon
She let the water run in the tub
lay back and slowly slashed both wrists
with a plastic razor

She was singing
It was her birthday.
She had turned 62.
She had locked the bathroom door

Her husband pushed it open
and rushed in —
his wife slumped
in the bright red water of the tub

She was rushed to the hospital
She lived to tell me that story
Now 76

"I had every reason
to die, but I didn't ..."

When she was six
her own mother had thrown herself
into a deep ravine on Bathurst Street
Her maternal grandmother
one late night coming back
from a poker game in Tecumseh
was killed
when a freight train slammed
into her Buick at a railway crossing
Her younger sister
vacationing out west with her fiancé
after a night of drinking
drowned at dawn in a motel pool

"I had every reason
to die, but I didn't."

Somehow it seemed right that morning
as she gazed
at her sudden nakedness in crimson water
—like the beginning, but now the end
singing happiness alive

"I lived to tell that story, but why?"

GUARDIAN ANGEL

He's lazy and never around
when I need him
I drive down
to the coffee shop
in the early morning
and find him reading the paper
or talking to the locals

I want to tell him
he's not taking this seriously
— he's supposed to watch over me

He shrugs and says the rules
have changed
I can reach him on Facebook
Besides he carries a cell phone

I want to ask how he got this job
Why me? Why him?
Luck of the draw, he shrugs
our birthdays the same
we both have bad eyes
a hearing problem
and can't eat spicy foods

But where was he in October 1950
the afternoon on Wyandotte
when I was four
and I ran between
two parked cars?
He was there, he says
coming out of the pool hall
to save me
to cup my bleeding head

on the warm pavement
to glare at the driver
who stood in the open door
of his Ford worried sick
that I might die

He was there, he said
otherwise I might not
be having this conversation
and he was there again
when I lay curled up
and unconscious
in the hospital room one winter
swearing at the hospital staff
after bowel surgery
and he touched my lips
with his index and middle fingers
and quieted me

Besides, he's always there
and there's no point
having this conversation
— he's so far ahead
and knows so much more:
a hundred different languages
names of every star
in the universe, the physics
of flying, and the winner
of the Stanley Cup
every year till the
end of time

NO LAZY BONES

I'm no lazy bones,
I'm a busy man, I work all day
the man shouts as he shuffles
in sunlight outside
this sprawling but empty
72-passenger school bus
parked in a desolate church lot
at Michigan and Trumbull

A fire rages in a nearby barbecue pit
as he feeds it cardboard boxes
and Sunday's *Free Press*
and assures me the men will keep warm
huddled tonight around
the back of the bus
that's going nowhere

The word *Democracy*
is emblazoned across
the whole side of the bus
shouts out to the vacant street
and to the man
who roams free in the open space
of this lumbering creature
that looms like T. rex over
a barren urban landscape

I'm no lazy bones,
I'm a busy man, I work all day

THE UNDERPAINTING

For Ken Saltmarche and Russell Farrow

The young man painted a forest
over the mayor's bedroom walls —
Sumacs, Red Bud, Yellow Birch,
Mulberry, Witchhazel
Dogwood, and Beech —muted stretches
of branches, green as spring,
and a sky spreading its way as
hands softly through hair
And the young man went away
happy to be paid, and the mayor
woke each day to a dazzling forest
in morning light, and knew
the days were right

After a long while, the mayor
passed away and the house was sold
and others came and went
and the forest bloomed each morning
and others woke to its brilliant light
of Yellow Birch, Beech and Mulberry

till another moved in one dull-gray day
maybe spooked by the forest
its branches or the gaps of clear blue sky
maybe fearful of the past
or ghosts that live in such swirls of green
and so he painted it over

At night — so the story goes,
the mayor and the painter, both long dead
wend their way down the solitary street
and climb the stairs to the upper bedroom
and together hear the wind in the Dogwood
and feel the luster of light

6

GRACE OF PRAYER

THE INNOCENT

For Peter and Denise Hrastovec

There is nothing you could know
of a boy who sleeps in a dream
and glides with the grace of prayer

My friends, hear his plea,
see the story, see his face
see the streets in which he plays

see the boy who sails on hope
through streets that you don't know

see the boy who glides with ease
of day-long joy, see the dream
that he can't know

see him glide with the grace of prayer
that sets his face aglow

My friends, there is nothing you can see
unless you find the words to say

there's a dream, there's a boy,
there's a prayer, there's a way
to find the streets that sing that joy
otherwise glide with the grace of prayer

and find the boy who sleeps in a dream.